THE OJ SIMPSON TRIAL

THE OJ SIMPSON TRIAL

a collection

by

Ronald Williams

Rev. date: 09/13/2013

To order additional copies of this book, contact:
Xlibris Corporation
1-888-795-4274
www.Xlibris.com
Orders@Xlibris.com
132777

CONTENTS

THE O.J. SIMPSON MYSTERY

Who? What? Why? When?

Part I

While sitting in the Greyhound Bus Terminal in Albany, New York, in June of 1994, working on my novel, I decided to buy a *Sunday Times Union* newspaper to read about the O.J. Simpson murder case. While at the rack, a strange man walked over and bought a newspaper. He stood beside me, looking at his newspaper, then over at me.

Maybe the person knew or saw something where they thought O.J. was being used, being taken advantage of. Maybe this friend thought O.J. Simpson was a victim of abuse and went to Nicole's home and murdered her and Ron Goldman.

It might have been an old love or date who was seeing Nicole when O.J. was out of town on business trips, someone who became jealous of Nicole seeing Ron Goldman and knew O.J. and Nicole were having problems. So that person murdered Nicole and set O.J. up, knowing O.J. would be convicted of the crime.

"Just look at the way the murder was committed. It had to be someone full of hate to murder two people in a mean, vicious, and savage way: to slash and stab someone; to cut the victims all over their bodies. That was deep—down hate.

No man in his right mind who loved a woman, married her, and then had children by that woman would cut her neck. No matter how big the problem—then try to cut her breast from her body, slash and stab her—even if she was his ex-wife.

That was a savage murder.

"Now does that make sense? Not at all, I say, if you know O.J. Simpson. If you use logic and analyze the whole crime, it just doesn't fit O.J. I'm telling you this so you can write about it and let the world know they have the wrong man in jail."

The stranger hesitated, then said, "I'm going to catch my bus to New York now."

After the strange man walked off, I said to myself, 'That man's crazy. WHY would he tell me all that?' After coming home, I settled down to think about what the stranger had told me.

Hearing/seeing the murder on TV and reading about the case in the newspaper, if you take time to analyze the crime, according to some of the things the stranger told me about the Simpson and Goldman slaying that day at the Albany Bus Terminal, the strange man seems to be right about a lot of what he said.

The man, dressed in green fatigues and a black beret, was approximately 5′9″ tall, weighing about 190 pounds, with a black beard. He looked like he might belong to the Green Berets.

He said to me, "I was watching you. Are you a writer?"

I replied, "Yes," to the stranger.

"Well," the man said as he looked at his newspaper again with O.J. Simpson's picture on the front page. "O.J. didn't murder those people. I just left Los Angeles and whoever committed the murder must have been an expert with weapons. The detectives should be looking for someone with experience who was trained to murder. It had to be someone who moved fast, knew all the fatal and disabling points of the body, and used a weapon to cut the throat and other parts of the body by slashing and stabbing. The weapon might have been a knife or some kind of sword. Whoever murdered O.J.'s ex-wife and Ron Goldman was an expert in the martial arts.

"And another thing was the way the killing went down. While using the weapon to cut Nicole, she could have grabbed the knife or sword, whichever one was used, when trying to fight the attacker, pulling off the left glove. And after the murder, WHO would have known to go out the back alley to get away from the murder scene? It had to be someone who knew Nicole's residence very well. That part was planned. They had to have an extra set of keys to drive the Ford Bronco if no other kind of transportation was used to get to the Simpson home.

"A blue stocking cap was left. Was there black or blond hair in that cap? A bloody glove, a beeper, and an envelope were all left at the murder scene. Upon reaching the Simpson home, the person went over the fence and past the dog in the yard. Don't you think it had to be someone the dog knew?

"How about this person trying to get into a window but failing, dropping the bloody glove while going back across the fence past the dog again. The murderer must have known the only way to get inside the Simpson house was by the front door—not seeing the limousine parked at the Simpson residence waiting to carry O.J. Simpson to the airport.

"That's not all. Could it have been a close relative with the same blood type? You know, there were blood droppings found. Maybe it was someone else, someone loyal who had become attached to O.J."

Part II—Questions

Question—WHO was the murder of Nicole Brown Simpson and Ronald Goldman? With all the blood found in the yard of Nicole Simpson, WHAT kind of weapon was used to kill them?

Question—WHAT time of day was it when the murder took place? Did a man or woman have something to do with these mystery killings? WHAT about the Ford Bronco? After seeing all the blood at Nicole's home, WHY wasn't there more blood on the inside and outside of the Ford Bronco rather than just on the door handle?

Question—How could a person drop all of those spots of blood in the yard from such a small cut on their hand, like the one that was on O.J. Simpson's hand? That cut was not big enough to drop those spots.

About that bloody glove: While trying to fight off the attacker, whoever the killer was that committed the murder of Nicole Simpson and Ronald Goldman, wouldn't the left glove have to be cut or have some kind of scratches on it if Nicole tried to grab the weapon with her hand?

What about this? There was one glove found at the murder scene; another glove discovered at the home of O.J. Simpson. When the L.A.P.D. people started their investigation, the question is how did that left glove get from the murder scene to the home of O.J. Simpson, lying in O.J.'s yard, if that was the murder glove used in the killing of Simpson and Goldman?

Question—To find the bloody glove in O.J. Simpson's yard where there are cameras around the home and a dog, wouldn't you think, if the cameras did not pick up something strange, would the dog have found the bloody glove and possibly moved it from place to place? It sounds like someone who knew the cameras were there, as well as the dog, who put or dropped that bloody left glove there to be found.

Now about the Ford Bronco—Wouldn't there have been more blood on the Ford Bronco than just a little drop if the murder used that vehicle to get away from the murder scene? If the murderer put that bloody glove in the Simpson yard, it was someone who really did not care about getting an innocent person convicted of a murder they did not commit.

What about the glove already at the murder scene? Someone found one glove in front of Nicole's home and another in the back near the alleyway. Maybe that person carried the left glove to O.J. Simpson's estate and after getting into the yard, claimed they found the glove in the yard of O.J. Simpson at the time of the investigation. What about this? If that bloody glove had'nt been found at O.J. Simpson's estate, what would they have come up with next. About the mystery of the bloody glove: We know at the time that bloody glove was lying around in the Simpson yard. To me that does not sound right. If some strange person went into O.J. Simpson's yard, why the dog was running around? Wouldn't the dog have bitten the person if it was a stranger who left that bloody glove in the yard? The whole glove matterdoesn't make sense.

Further about the Ford Bronco. If the vehicle was used in the crime, by whoever drove it, wouldn't there have been more blood on the door handle? And if the glove was found at the Simpson home, and the Ford had blood on it, what happened to the bloody clothes the murder was wearing? Don't forget the bloody shoes the murder was wearing. Wouldn't there have been some sign of blood on the floor of the Ford Bronco or in the yard of O.J.'s home? As for footprints from the bloody shoes, there were bloody footprints leading from the murder scene.

This is a mixed-up and confusing murder case, and nothing in the crime sounds right at all. The pieces just do not fit. It looks like the investigation of the murders of Nicole Simpson and Ronald Goldman needs to be started all over again. Maybe someone will come up with the right person who committed the slayings, because, believe it or not, the wrong man is locked up in jail. This crime just does not fit O.J. Simpson, one of America's great.

.   .   .

Part III

Month three after the death of Nicole Brown Simpson and Ronald Goldman from the beginning of the crime we are now going through the preliminary hearing to the end of the arraignment. Why is O.J. Simpson pleading innocent and fighting for his life? The question is, what were the motives? Why were Nicole and Simpson and Goldman murdered?

Who might have had a motive to kill those two people? Could it have been some kind of fear that someone had been hiding for a long time soon to be revealed? Could money have played a part in killing those people? Was there jealousy after O.J. and Nicole were divorced? Could it have been a person who thought they would be with Nicole, but she ended up with Ronald Goldman?

O.J. Simpson was a famous football star, loved playing golf, and was in the middle of making a new movie. Could one of those events have had some kind of connection to the murder?

What about that movie? Is there someone connected to that movie who might know something about the murder? The killing did not happen until that picture was being made. Are there some clues there? Ask yourself this question: Who is the guilty person who is trying to cover up the killing by misleading the authorities? Is it a man or woman the investigators would be looking for who committed the killings?

Further clues: Nicole was receiving threatening phone calls. Who could the stalker have been? Who was the person who called? O.J.'s baby daughter heard Nicole, and everyone with her, at the home the night of the slaying.

What about the blue stocking hat, beeper, bloody glove, and envelopes found at the murder scene? Where is the knife the killer used? Or was some other type of weapon used?

Question—I would like to know who the man was at Nicole's home the night O.J. Simpson came over and broke in the back door. Who was the man O.J. Simpson was fighting with at Nicole's home when you could hear O.J.'s voice over the answering machine? Why was Nicole calling 911 that night? I would like to know the man's name who was at Nicole's home when 911 was called, and the man O.J. Simpson's 8-year-old daughter heard the night of the murder at Nicole's home. Do the detectives know about the fight? Is there some kind of letter or postcard? Could there be some kind of clue lying around somewhere in the house? Was it a tap or message on the answering machine found at Nicole's home during the time of the L.A.P.D. investigation?

What about the bloody footprints found leading from the murder scene? Ask yourself again: Could those bloody footprints have been those of a man or woman?

Another question: A stranger could have been in the area that particular evening, and a robbery might have been involved in the crime. If robbery was the motive behind the murders, look at the crime in this way. How could a stranger know where O.J. Simpson lived, and to leave the murder scene carrying a bloody glove, and leave the bloody glove in O.J. Simpson's yard—that doesn't make sense. If a stranger was committing the robbery and had come into the back alley of Nicole's home, the person would have tried to slip in the back door or tried going in through a side window, knowing that if they tried to enter the front, someone would see them. I ask again: Why would the stranger, if a robbery was taking place at Nicole's home, kill two people, drop a beeper, leave a bloody glove, blue stocking cap, and envelopes? Would that robber, taking nothing from the robbery scene, then take time to drive over to O.J. Simpson's home, go over a fence where there is possibly a camera and a dog, not knowing that he dropped a bloody glove in O.J. Simpson's yard? Would the camera not have picked up something? Or would the dog not have bitten the stranger? So, failing to get in the house one way, could he have gone back past a dog again and over the fence without the camera picking his movement up or him getting bit? The person knows he can't get in the Simpson home one way, so he takes a chance of trying to use the front entrance of O.J. Simpson's estate. What was the stranger going to do when he got inside O.J.'s home, not knowing if he would run into some member of the family who lived in the home? I am telling you these movements will make you think that no robbery was going on in this crime at all.

Talking about the Simpson case and possible clues is an attempt to see this crime in a little clearer light, and where the murder mystery might make sense. Let's talk about the blood evidence; the blood sample; and what about the hair from O.J. Simpson that's needed to perform the tests? What if the blood and hair tests come back negative? Do you think this Simpson murder case will take a turn? I think so.

Let's take time to ask ourselves this question (because everybody should be in suspense by now wondering who the real killer is): Could it have been someone who wanted to kill Ronald Goldman, and Nicole got in the way? You also might want to ask: How could the murderer have known that Ronald Goldman was going to be at Nicole's home that particular evening? Had Goldman been followed by someone? Could the murderer have already been at Nicole Simpson's home for some reason, and when Ronald Goldman got there, he knew the murder was there to kill?

The question is, who would have known so much about Nicole and O.J.'s problem marriage to leave a bloody glove at O.J. Simpson's estate to cover up the murder? The answer to this murder is yet to be known. And whoever committed the slaying is still out there.

The authorities are working hard to solve the crime. O.J. Simpson, who used to be a free man, lives in confinement awaiting an answer that may free him, put him away for a long time, or take his life. But remember, this is America and in this country, a man is innocent until proven guilty.

.   .   .

Part IV—The Evidentiary Hearing

On August 22, 1994, O.J. Simpson and Al Cowling are going to court on different charges. Just because a life-long friend was trying to help another, O.J. Simpson is being blamed for a murder of ex-wife Nicole Brown Simpson and Ronald Goldman.

Not believing that this misfortune was happening to him, O.J. Simpson, after staying in his home and thinking about this crime that had taken the lives of ex-wife Nicole and Ronald Goldman, had to have some kind of open space—not to run from the law or resist arrest by the police, but just to get away to clear his head, to make a right decision. Best friend, Al Cowling, after possibly talking about the murder with O.J., decided to help his best friend in some way to keep him from cracking up. Like two good friends would do to keep the other one from suicide, the two took the Ford Bronco and drove to Los Angeles.

Why did O.J. hold a gun to his head lying down in the back seat of the Ford Bronco? Why did his best childhood friend drive around town to keep his friend from killing himself? For two best friends the time had come that June day to prove that long childhood friendship.

Let's look back at O.J. Simpson and Al Cowling growing up together as children in the Project in San Francisco. They attended the same elementary school and high school. Together, they went to college, going on to pro football together.

Now, O.J.'s good friend Al Cowling is going to court just for helping keep another person from killing himself. How many people who are supposed to be that close would have put their life on the line like Al Cowling did to help his best friend? Now O.J. Simpson is in jail and during the month of September the court is hearing the evidence in the case. The public still does not know who murdered the two people are reason why O.J. Simpson, a man who got his name in the Hall of Fame, now sits in court day by day listening to evidence against him.

After the evidence is heard in the Simpson case, it is time for O.J. to return to jail to wait until the next court hearing. O.J. no doubt is thinking that maybe the day will come when all of this misfortune will come to an end and he can say, "I am glad to be a free man once more. I can go back to my children."

While O.J. is waiting, the newspapers are keeping up with his daily life in jail. The newspapers reported O.J. Simpson getting sick in jail and that cancer might have been the problem. The newspapers also reported O.J. was taken to the hospital from the central jail in Los Angeles. The hospital is Cedars Sinai Medical Center near Beverly Hills, California. Upon being examined by a physician, a lump was found under O.J.'s armpit. A biopsy was performed and the lump was later removed by surgery, after which the doctor reported that O.J. was doing just fine. After release from the hospital, O.J. was returned to the main central jail in Los Angeles. There he will stay until his next evidence hearing.

While O.J. waited to go back to court, the newspapers reported that the DNA tests had come back and did not show any connection of O.J. to the crime. The tests were negative. The blood drops leading from the crime scene were not those of O.J. Simpson. The DNA tests were wrong. On television came a news report which said the information that was given out on the DNA tests were false; the blood drops found did match O.J.'s blood type. Now that piece of misinformation should make you think about this case. Many mistakes were made in the handling of the crime.

Later, another report came out that Nicole talked to her mother over the phone at 10:28 P.M. on the night of the murder. One would want to know: Was there a person at Nicole's home when she talked to her mother who knew Ronald Goldman was coming over to bring Nicole the glasses? The question is, can the time be determined? What time did the conversation take place between Nicole and her mother? Was the call made at 10 P.M. and no later than 11 P.M.? When was the murder committed and what time can be set that this crime took place at Nicole's home in June 1994? What is the truth in this murder case? Looking at the clues in this crime, you would want to know who the man was that Nicole was seen with at Ben and Jerry's ice cream place on the night of the crime.

Some further clues remain in this crime: Who could the murder have been who left a bloody glove and stocking cap at Ronald Goldman's feet? Could it have been someone who wanted you to know they were there to murder Ronald Goldman for some reason? What about the bloody footprints leading from the murder scene? Was the footprints large or small? What size shoe could have placed the print there? Who could have committed a crime like the Simpson and Goldman murder in such a short time? Could this person have been a big strong person who was right-handed, or is the murderer left-handed? Was he skilled in the use of a knife? Who could commit a murder like that and leave the crime scene so easily without someone seeing them? What time did the murder take place? Only Nicole's dog saw the murderer. When Nicole and the children were seen at Ben and Jerry's, Who was the man with them? Had someone left Nicole's home, then come back and found Ronald Goldman there with her? Is jealousy the motive?

Why did this murder happen? Was the murder to protect a loved one? Who could have masterminded this crime? What time did Ronald Goldman arrived with Nicole's sunglasses? Or did the killer drive the vehicle? Or was someone waiting to carry off the killer's clothes and the knife? Could two people be involved in this crime?

You might ask: What happened to the bloody clothes and shoes and murderer was wearing that made the footprints which led from the scene of the crime? Where is the knife that the murderer used to murder the two people? Do you think this murder puzzle will ever be put together?

Let's take a clear look at this murder puzzle that everyone is trying to put together. Why was the bloody glove left at Ronald Goldman's feet, then a trial of blood found leading to O.J.'s home, where another bloody glove was found in the yard that matched the glove left at the murder scene? Where did the blood drops in O.J. Simpson's driveway come from? How could all that blood be dropped from a small cut like the one on O.J.'s hand. Then, after dropping all that blood, he would go get on an airplane for Chicago? Seems like the bleeding would have stopped by then. I can see how the man could break a glass and cut his hand when the call was made telling him that his ex-wife was murdered. I could see him going through pain and doing something like that. You can see how the blood got on the sheet in the hotel room. So, between the bloody trail and the blood on the Ford Bronco, it is impossible the blood evidence could have happened that way.

I am suspicious about the blood trail. If there was a struggle and the stocking cap and glove were pulled off the head and hand of the murderer, then why were they left at the scene of the crime? What is the reason? I ask again: Could the motive in this murder be jealousy? I want to know who killed those two people and was trying to put the murder on O.J. Simpson.

Again, let's look at the clues in this crime and the way the whole murder was set up. Who is the real murderer who is throwing the investigators off the trail? I want to know who could mastermind such a terrible murder and put the blame on another person. They must be dangerous. Have the detectives discovered the reason there is so much confusion in this case?

I am in suspense and would like to know: Who are the other suspects outside of O.J. Simpson? Are other people being interviewed in this case? Did the detectives notice any behavior that would give them an idea that one of the suspects being interviewed might be capable of murder? Do all the suspects have credible alibis as to where they were on the night of the murder? After all that has been said about this murder, when will the real truth be told? Do you think we will ever find out who the person is that committed the murder when the trial gets under way and all the evidence comes out?

Let's not forget about the notebook that was found. Is there something in the notebook that may have some connection to clues? Can a motive be found in that book? What about the receipt for gas that was found in the

Ford Bronco when the vehicle was searched? Are there clues hidden in those parts of the evidence that could tell us who might have had a motive for murder? Is everything dependent on the DNA evidence?

How about the blood test? How wrong was the inspecting and gathering the blood? Do you think the blood evidence was handled in the right way by the LAPD criminalist at the crime scene? At O.J. Simpson's home, was the blood investigation done in a professional way? Can you say in your mind, if it is determined that this is the right blood, that the blood was not dropped there a long time ago? Is the prosecutor going to give the defense team some evidence so the defense can determine if the blood found at the murder scene is that of O.J. Simpson?

It should be noted that there are no witnesses to the crime, the detectives do not have a knife or any other weapon; all they have is that DNA blood evidence.

After all the mistakes made in gathering the blood samples, do you think the court should let the blood evidence be used in the case? Do you think the evaluation of the blood samples was handled so as to connect O.J. Simpson to this crime?

I am in suspense. I want to know if the judge is going to make a ruling to throw out the blood evidence. Will the yellow sealed envelope be opened? I want to know what is in the envelope. Is there a knife like the one O.J. bought before the crime happened?

When O.J. goes back to court, a judge will be picked to try the case. Will this judge let the prosecutor keep the blood evidence? Will the notebook play a big part in the case? What about the stolen car that belonged to O.J.'s girlfriend?

Let's talk about the notebook again. Why should someone keep a list of a person's whereabouts? How long did this stalking act go on? I would like to know why O.J.'s girlfriend would keep a notebook on Nicole Simpson. Could this be some kind of motive connected to the murder?

Let's talk more about the blood that was sent to a lab. Do you think the other DNA tests will come back negative or positive?

Before we move on to the evidence hearing, let's not forget about the coroner's reports made on the bodies of Nicole Simpson and Ronald Goldman. Do you think the coroner's investigation into the murder was handled in a professional way?

After all the mistakes that have been made in the evidence gathering, do you think O.J. Simpson can get a fair trial? That is a question everyone should ask themselves after reading and hearing all that is being printed and said about this crime.

Let's not forget about the hair sample taken from O.J. Simpson's head to be examined by the prosecutor to determine if it matches the hair found at the crime scene. What do you think about the hair? I wonder if the hair is O.J.'s or someone else's. Where was the hair found—on the ground or in the blue stocking cap that the murderer left?

Today someone said on television that Judge Lance Ito will preside at the trial. Ito is the husband of a captain in the L.A.P.D. After hearing the DNA blood evidence in court today, Judge Ito made a ruling to keep the yellow sealed envelope and the blood samples for evidence. Does the prosecution think they have something now to go on that might bring the guilty person to justice? What if the DNA test that was sent to a lab in Maryland comes back positive? Do you think that Judge Ito will make a ruling so the defense team can do their own DNA test so the trial will be fair? Will the prosecutor give the defense team some of the blood to do their own testing to determine for themselves that the blood drops are that of O.J. Simpson without a reasonable doubt?

There is no mistake that the blood is the same type as that of O.J. Simpson, but then again you would wonder: Could the blood drops be someone else's who has the same type blood as O.J. Simpson?

Could the blood be that of another person? Well, the prosecutor and the defense team will talk about the blood tests today. The evidentiary trial has started.

As I listen to the TV news and read my daily paper, these dozens of questions haunt me. Will we *really* learn the truth when the trial begins? If we, as good Americans, believe in our system of justice (and it is the only one we have), then we must all hope and pray that in this strange and unusual case, Justice will, indeed, triumph!

.   .   .

Target And Clues

Let's first talk about the perpetrator in the Simpson murder case.

We have O.J. Simpson as the suspect in the Nicole Brown Simpson and the Ron Goldman murders.

But let's analyze the crime and use some logic in trying to figure out the mystery of the Simpson and Goldman slayings. Let's backtrack and say it was two gloves the killer left at the crime scene under that bush and Ron Goldman was the target.

Now let's start the investigation from the restaurant where Ron Goldman worked and assume that when Nicole Brown made the telephone call to Ron Goldman while he was at work, someone was in Nicole's home listening to her talk to Ron. Could this person have been involved with Nicole somehow and have gotten jealous when she started seeing Ron?

Let's assume the person, after hearing the conversation, left Nicole's condo angry, went and got the gloves, the knit cap, and a knife and came back, knowing Ron was on his way to Nicole's condo. What if the person waited for them behind the tall plants in the yard and when Nicole came out of the house when Ron Goldman arrived, the killer attacked them while standing between Nicole and Ron. What if the killer at first was talking to the two victims.

Now let's look at the crime in another way. Did someone at the restaurant hear the telephone call asking Ron to bring the sunglasses? Maybe Ron was involved with that person, who got upset when Ron started having visits at the restaurant with Nicole. Did this person see that night a window of opportunity and follow Ron Goldman to Nicole Brown Simpson's condo and murder them both out of jealousy and anger?

Now let's look at this crime in yet another way. A report said that Ron went somewhere after he left the restaurant and had a meal before he went to Nicole Brown Simpson's house. Could that meal have been with someone Ron was seeing who didn't like Ron and Nicole's relationship, who said that if she couldn't have Ron, no other woman would? Could that person have followed Ron to Nicole's house and killed Ron Goldman and Nicole Brown Simpson? Or was someone still following Ron from the restaurant? Whether Ron had the meal with a woman or a man could be a clue to the killing.

If you look at the way Nicole Brown was murdered—her throat slashed, stab wounds to the body, the breast cut—it would seem that the perpetrator was a person who disliked women. And Ron's injuries—his throat slashed, stabbed in the fatal nerve center, from the waist down—a paralyzing display.

You might wonder if the killer knew something about martial arts in view of the strategy that was used on the two victims. The way Nicole was cut could be a clue as to whether the killer was a man or woman.

Let's talk about the restaurant work, modeling jobs, and the acting Ron was into. Could there be some connection between his work and the murders? Someone should look into Rons' background all over again.

The murderer left the glove and knit cap at Ron Goldman's feet. Why weren't they left by Nicole Brown's body? Was Ron Goldman the target?

The police investigation revealed blood in and outside the Ford Bronco, meaning that the vehicle could have been used in the crime. But let's look at the blood trail. A spot was discovered on the vehicle and there were blood drops going from the Ford Bronco onto O.J. Simpson's driveway, and up to the house. If there was blood leading from the Ford Bronco up to the house, why didn't the blood trail go around the side path? Why wasn't blood found coming or going from the front to the rear of O.J. Simpson's yard.?

If the guilty person jumped over the side fence, blood drops should have been discovered going and coming from the rear to the front of O.J. Simpson's property, but the blood trail was cut off at the front of the house.

If you look at the space between the blood found in the front of the house and the glove in the rear, you might ask yourself if that bloody glove was placed in O.J. Simpson's yard by someone. Then, you might ask another question—did O.J. Simpson murder Nicole Brown and Ronald Goldman or is the real murderer still out there somewhere.

What is the answer to the mystery of

WHO? WHAT? WHY? WHEN?

The O.J. Simpson Murder Mystery—Part 2

Who—What—Why—When
The Bloody Glove

Question—Who was the murderer of Nicole Brown Simpson and Ronald Goldman? With all of the blood that was found in the yard of Nicole Simpson, what kind of weapon was used to kill them?

Question—What time of day was it when the murder took place? Did a man or woman have something to do with these mystery killings; and what about the Ford Bronco—after seeing all the blood at Nicole's home, why wasn't there more blood on the inside and outside of the Ford Bronco rather than just on the vehicle door handle?

Question—How could a person drop all of those spots of blood on the yard from such a small cut on their hand, like the one that was on O.J. Simpson's hand? That cut was not big enough.

Let's talk about the bloody glove. While trying to fight off the attacker, whoever the killer was that committed the murder of Nicole Simpson and Ronald Goldman, wouldn't the left glove have to be cut or have some kind of scratches on it if Nicole tried to grab the weapon with her hand?

What about this: there was one glove found at the murder scene; another glove discovered at the home of O.J. Simpson. When the L.A.P.D. people started their investigation, the question is how did that left glove get from the murder scene to the home of O.J. Simpson and laying in O.J.'s yard if that was the murder glove that was used in the killing of Nicole Simpson and Ron Goldman?

Question—Now, to find the bloody glove in O.J. Simpson's yard where there are cameras around the home, and a dog. Wouldn't you think, if the cameras didn't pick something strange up, would the dog have found the bloody glove and possibly move it from place to place. It sounds like someone close, who knew that the cameras were there as well as the dog, that put or dropped that bloody left glove there to be found.

Let's talk about the Ford Bronco some more—wouldn't there have been more blood on the Ford Bronco than just a little drop if the murderer used that Ford Bronco to get away from the murder scene? The way those two people were murdered—all of the blood found at the home of Nicole Simpson. It was a lot. And if the murderer put the bloody glove in the Simpson yard, that was someone who really didn't care about getting an innocent person convicted of a murder they didn't commit. Just for their own gain. Now, what about the glove already at the murder scene, and someone found one glove in the front of Nicole's home and another glove in the back where the alleyway was. Maybe that person carried the left glove to O.J. Simpson's estate, and after getting into the yard, claiming they found the glove in the yard of O.J. Simpson at the time of the investigation.

What about this: if that bloody glove hadn't been found at O.J. Simpson's estate, what would they have come up with next? Now the mystery of the bloody glove. You know at the time, that bloody glove was laying around and in the Simpson yard the dog didn't mess with the bloody glove. To me that don't sound right. If some strange person went into O.J. Simpson's yard, why the dog was running around—wouldn't the dog have bitten the person if it was a stranger that left that bloody glove in that yard? It just doesn't make sense. The whole murder case.

Let's talk about the Ford Bronco some more. If the Ford Bronco was used in the murder crime, whoever drove the vehicle—that's if the Ford Bronco was use doing the murder—wouldn't there have been more blood on the door handle? And if the glove was found at the Simpson home, and there was the Ford with blood on it, well what happened to the bloody clothes the murderer was wearing, and don't forget about the bloody shoes the murderer was wearing.

Wouldn't there have been some sign of blood on the floor of the Ford Bronco or in the yard of O.J. Simpson's home?

As for foot prints from the bloody shoes, you know, there were bloody foot prints leading from the murder scene. You know, this is a mixed up and confusing murder case, and nothing in the crime sounds right at all. The pieces just don't fit. Looks like the investigation of Nicole Brown Simpson and Ronald Goldman needs to be started all over again from the beginning, and maybe someone will come up with the right person that committed the slayings, because believe it or not, the wrong man is locked up in jail. This crime just doesn't fit O.J. Simpson, one of America's greatest.

The O.J. Simpson Murder Mystery—Part 3

Who—What—Why—When

Month three after the death of Nicole Brown Simpson and Ronald Goldman from the beginning of the crime—now going through the preliminary hearing to the end of the arraignment, why is O.J. Simpson pleading and fighting for his life, not guilty of the murder of Nicole Brown Simpson and Ronald Goldman. Now the question is, what were the motives? Why was Nicole Brown Simpson and Ronald Goldman murdered?

Let's talk about who might have had a motive to kill those two people. Could it have been some kind of fear that someone could be hiding for long and soon would be revealed. Or was there jealousy after O.J. Simpson and Nicole Simpson were divorced. Could it have been a person who thought they would be with Nicole, but she ended up with Ronald Goldman.

Another thing to think about. As you know, O.J. Simpson was a famous football star and loved playing golf, and now was in the middle of making a new movie. Could one of those events have had some kind of connection to Nicole Simpson and Ronald Goldman being murdered? What about the movie? Is there someone connected to that movie that might know something about that murder? You know, the killing didn't happen until that picture was being made. Are there some clues there? Or you might ask yourself this question—whoever is the guilty person that's trying to cover up their killing by misleading the authorities—is it a man or woman, that the investigator should be looking for, that committed the killing?

How about some more clues. You know, Nicole was receiving threatening phone calls. Now who could the stalker have been, and who was that person? O.J.'s baby daughter heard Nicole talking to, at the home the night of the slaying.

Let's talk some more about clues in the Simpson and Goldman murder case. What about the blue stocking hat, beeper, the bloody glove, and envelopes that were found at the murder scene. Now where is the knife that the killer used? Or was it some other type of weapon used in the murders?

Question—I would like to know who was the man at Nicole Brown Simpson's home the night O.J. Simpson came over and broke the back door in. Who was the man O.J. Simpson was fighting with at Nicole's home—and you could hear O.J.'s voice over the answering machine. Why was Nicole calling on 911 that night? I am in suspense. I would like to know the man's name that was at Nicole Simpson's home when 911 was called, and the man that O.J. Simpson's 8-year-old daughter heard the night of the murder at Nicole Brown Simpson's. Now do the detectives know about the fight? Is there some kind of letter or post card? Could there be some kind of clue laying around somewhere in the house? Was it a tap or message on the answering machine found at the home of Nicole Brown Simpson during the time of the L.A.P.D. investigation?

Now what about the bloody foot prints found leading from the murder scene? Ask yourself again—could those bloody foot prints have been a man or woman?

Now another question to ask—a stranger could have been in the area that particular evening, and a robbery might have been involved in that crime. Well what about this; if a robbery had been the motive behind Nicole Brown Simpson's and Ronald Goldman's murder. Look at the crime in this way. how would a stranger know where O.J. Simpson lived, and to leave the murder scene carrying a bloody glove, and leave the bloody glove in O.J. Simpson's yard—that doesn't make sense. Looks like as if a stranger was committing the robbery, and the robber had come into the back alley of Nicole Simpson's home, the person would have tried to slip in the back door or try going in through a side window, knowing that if they tried to enter the front, someone would see them.

That's not all. I ask again, why would the stranger, if a robbery was taking place at Nicole Simpson's home, kill two people, drop a beeper, leave a bloody glove, blue stocking cap and envelopes. And that robber, taking nothing from the robbery scene, then takes time to drive over to O.J. Simpson's home, go over a fence where there is possibly a camera and a dog, not knowing that he dropped a bloody glove in O.J. Simpson's yard. Wouldn't the camera have picked something up? Or wouldn't the dog have bitten the stranger? So, failing to get in the house one way, go back past a dog again and over the fence, without the camera picking their movement up or getting bit. Now the person knows they can't get in the Simpson home one way, so they take a chance of trying to go use the front entrance of O.J. Simpson's estate. Now what was the stranger going to do when he got inside O.J.'s home, not knowing if they would run into some member that lived in the home? I am telling you their movement will make you think there wasn't a robbery going on in this crime at all.

Now after talking about the Simpson case and possible clues, trying to see this crime a little clearer in the light, and where that murder mystery might make sense. Let's not forget to talk about the blood evidence; the blood sample; and what about the hair from O.J. Simpson that's going to be needed to perform the tests. What if the blood and hair tests come back in a negative way? Do you think this Simpson murder case will take a turn? I would think so. Let's take time to ask ourselves this question (because everybody should be in suspense by now wondering who is the real killer) and now could it have been someone who wanted to kill Ronald Goldman and Nicole Brown Simpson got in the way. You also might want to know how would the murderer have known that Ronald Goldman was going to be at Nicole's home that particular evening. Had Ronald Goldman been followed by someone, or could the murderer have already been at Nicole Brown Simpson's home for some reason, and when Ronald Goldman got there, he knew the murderer was there to kill.

The question is, who would have known so much about Nicole Simpson's and O.J. Simpson's problem marriage to go and leave a bloody glove at O.J. Simpson's estate to cover this Simpson and Goldman murder up. The answer to this murder is yet to be known. Whoever committed the slaying is still out there. The authorities are still working hard to solve the Simpson and Goldman murder crime.

Now O.J. Simpson, who used to be a free man, lives in confinement waiting on an answer that may free him, put im away for a long time, or take his life. Now remember, this is America and in this country, a man is innocent until proven guilty.

Tampering And Clues Vision

The Missing Dirt

Where is the dirt that was suppose to be on the socks if there was a fight in Nicole Brown's yard?

Before I went to sleep last night—the DNA blood evidence—I saw it all. So I decided to write my vision down.

Now how about the DNA blood evidence. Let's backtrack and see what we will come up with, starting with the blood vial and the blood on the outside of that glass tube. How could a Q-tip be used to spot that blood? Let's point out the missing part—a 1.5 swatch can go a long way take out of a tube. Now they say it looks like everywhere O.J. Simpson's blood was found the blood was shown to be placed in a spot. At Nicole Brown's condo—on the walkway and rear gate—the Ford Bronco, the driveway, in the foyer.

Now look, the stairs were missed, and no blood going into the master bedroom, no blood spots on the door, the bed, clothing, or carpet.

But weeks later, blood found on the socks.

Now let's stop and look at the bloody socks and the clues to the socks evidence.

The picture diagram from Cellmark Lab and the Justice Department showed blood stains on the lower part of the socks that belonged to Nicole

Brown and the upper and lower parts of the socks that O.J. Simpson's blood match—and Nicole Brown.

Now look at the way the DNA scientist said the blood got on those socks. The killer had to be walking in Nicole Brown's blood and the blood splashed on the foot, socks, and inner leg up.

Well, what do you think about this? How could Nicole and O.J. Simpson's blood get on the sock the way the DNA blood criminalist said if the killer had on pants.

I am talking about the blood stain that was found at the top part of the sock.

THE CLUES TO THE SOCK

Now do you want to know the clues to the sock?

The socks are knee socks. How could blood get up that high on a sock walking. Did someone put blood strains at the top part of the sock? Was the blood evidence set up and then sent to the Cellmark Lab and Justice Department knowing the test and examination would show a mixture of Nicole Brown, Ron Goldman and O.J. Simpson's blood types. Would you say the Cellmark Lab and Justice Department were used in some way/

Now that's not all. The real part that's missing is there was a fight between Ron Goldman and the killer in Nicole Brown Simpson's yard.

Now look, where Ron Goldman and the perpetrator were fighting there was dry dirt and dust.

Wouldn't you think the dirt and dust would have gotten on the killer's shoes and socks like the criminalist said the blood did? You know those socks have been examined and none of the criminalist's have said anything about dirt being on those socks.

REASONABLE DOUBT

The dirt and the hole made in Nicole Brown's yard while the fight went on between Ron Goldman and the killer are the clues to O.J. Simpson's innocence.

You know all of the mistakes that were made in the evidence investigation. Something is wrong and the way the evidence was handled is strange.

Let's keep an open mind so we won't miss the truth of; Who, why, and when.

I would like to know where the dirt is that was supposed to be on those socks.

When I hear the answer, I will rest my case.

Now, is that Reasonable Doubt?

Thank you
Ronald Williams

.   .   .

KEEPING AN OPEN MIND UNTIL THE SIMPSON AND GOLDMAN MURDERS ARE SOLVED

Looking into this Simpson murder case:

Number one—how the investigation was handled, the way blood was collected, the police jumping the gun and going after O.J. Simpson as the suspect, blood being taken from O.J. Simpson then blood spots found in different places in the Ford Bronco, little stains leading from the door handle up to O.J. Simpson's house in to the front door.

Now what happened to the blood between the stairs going up to the master bedroom. The sock was found on the carpet with blood spots on it, but no blood spots on the side of the house in the path or on the fence.

And tell me, how could that little cut on O.J.'s hand drop all that blood?

What about the blood that was taken from O.J. Simpson? When the blood was turned into the lab, was all the blood there or had some been taken out of the tube and put in little places around the murder scene? And was Nicole Brown and Ronald Goldman's blood mixed and put n places in and from the crime scene?

Did anyone check to see if any of O.J. Simpson's blood was unaccounted for?

You know the public should be reminded to keep an open mind every day and ask themselves: Who knew Ronald Goldman was going to Nicole Brown's house that night? Is that the clue?

And the way the evidence and crime scene has been handled. Is the wrong person in jail?

Another question you should ask yourself: If O.J. Simpson killed Nicole Brown and Ronald Goldman, how would O.J. have known that Ronald Goldman was going to be at Nicole's condo?

CLEAR O.J. SIMPSON'S NAME

Let the jury know about the dust, blood, hole, dirt. Now those socks are clean. You know they think O.J. Simpson wore those socks over to Nicole Brown's house and killed Nicole Brown and Ron Goldman.

Why don't the defense and prosecution send those socks to the FBI Lab in Washington, D.C. and have the socks analyzed to see if there is dust or dirt that matches the dirt that's in Nicole Brown's yard?

Everything about the DNA and EDTA evidence and other things in the investigation are not falling in place.

Now Ron Goldman and the killer had a big fight in Nicole Brown's yard. The killer had to step in the blood if he moved fast, back and forward, between Nicole Brown Simpson and Ron Goldman the way those two people were cut and stabbed.

Maybe the jury needs to know about the dust and dirt.

You know, from looking at the Simpson trial on TV, the little things are the ones that made a big difference. Things like that are what the jury wants to know, and evidence like the dust is what the jurors want to see.

The jury is hearing everything else. So tell the jury about the dirt. That part of the trial might make those people sitting on the jury stand think that maybe the police have the wrong man.

You know other people see things that some people don't.

Thank you
Ron Williams

WHY THE JURORS FOUND O.J. SIMPSON NOT GUILTY

The jurors have talked out in television interviews answering questions and explaining to the public why they found O.J. Simpson *Not Guilty*. When asked about the verdict by a late night television host, a juror said there was too much reasonable doubt in the Simpson murder case and that police detectives handled the crime investigation wrong. Jurors told the public about the coroner coming to the crime scene late and that there was no right time of death; that the coroner threw the stomach contents of the victims away; that the coroner didn't know if the perpetrator used a single or double blade knife; and that there were problems with the coroner's autopsy report.

The jurors said the police walked over evidence at the crime scene and touched items before the evidence could be dusted for fingerprints and that the police looked at some items of evidence, such as the ice cream cup, and didn't test them for fingerprints. Jurors said mistakes were made, like the blood and other evidence found on Nicole Simpson's back gate being collected weeks later. They said the blood was contaminated and handled wrong by the police criminalist. The jurors explained that the detectives carried blood around for hours when it should have been booked at the police department right away for evidence.

The jurors asked, if the police didn't look at O.J. Simpson as a suspect, why did the detective jump over O.J. Simpson's fence before getting a search warrant. The jurors said they saw a Rush to Judgement by police detectives to think O.J. Simpson was the perpetrator. The jurors explained that there was a problem with blood missing from the vial the police had. They asked themselves what happened to that blood.

The jurors explained there was blood in little spots on the Ford Bronco, the gloves, the pair of socks, the doorway, but asked why it stopped in O.J. Simpson's front foyer and why there was no blood going up the stairway into O.J. Simpson's master bedroom where the socks were found. The jurors said there was no blood on the bed or carpet or on the fence or grass in the passageway where the detective found the bloody glove.

The jurors said they were trying to put the pieces together about the bloody glove and then later in the trial they found out that the police detective who had jumped O.J. Simpson's fence and come across the bloody glove on the side of O.J. Simpson's rear house was a bad police detective with a racist background who had a history of calling Black people the "N" word, who talked about beating Blacks and Hispanics and making up reasons to stop Black/White couples in their cars, setting them up, and taking their driver's licenses while he was on duty.

The jurors said they had a problem with the crime scene where the perpetrator and Ronald Goldman had a fight. The detectives' report said there was a hole made in the yard while the killer and Ronald Goldman were fighting. The jurors asked, if there was blood stains on the socks, why didn't the police lab find some dirt from Nicole Simpson's yard on them.

The jurors went on to say that Nicole Simpson had blood under her fingernails, which made it seem that she may have scratched the perpetrator. The jurors said they saw pictures of O.J. Simpson's body when he was examined by a doctor right after he was arrested and there were no marks or scratches to indicate he had been in a fight or struggle with anyone.

The jurors explained that the bag that the police said O.J. Simpson carried the bloody clothing and knife in was examined by the police lab and there was no blood stains on or in the bag to say that bloody clothing or a bloody knife had been in it. The jurors also said the police reported that O.J. Simpson had a Swiss type knife which he bought earlier that month which might have been used to murder his ex-wife Nicole Simpson and Ronald Goldman. There was a vanilla envelope that the Court held for evidence and didn't open at any time during the trial and the jurors said the knife that the police said O.J. Simpson had used to kill two people was in that envelope.

Then the jurors said the gloves that the killer used in the crime were old and worn and the jurors saw a problem with O.J. Simpson keeping a pair of old gloves.

The jurors explained that there was supposed to be a mountain of evidence that the D.A. had against O.J. Simpson and said that the D.A.'s office put on a good case, but a lot of evidence just didn't fit the crime. The jurors said there was no bloody clothing, no bloody shoes or knife, and no fingerprints found in the Simpson murder investigation to prove that O.J. Simpson went across town, cut up two people and killed them, changed clothes, and drove back to his Rockingham house in a short time and without anyone seeing him in that white Ford Bronco.

The jurors saw all the evidence in the Simpson murder trial, heard all the testimony, and took notes as they sat in the jury box for nine months.

They talked about the domestic abuse matter and came to the decision that the domestic problems took place a long time back in O.J. Simpson and Nicole Simpson's marriage, and they didn't think the domestic abuse meant that O.J. Simpson would have killed his ex-wife, Nicole Brown Simpson, and Ronald Goldman.

The jurors said they saw a number of mistakes and something wrong in the Simpson police investigation, and they had to go by Judge Lance Ito's instructions that if there was reasonable doubt, they must find O.J. Simpson not guilty of murdering Nicole Brown Simpson and Ronald Goldman.

The jurors said they wanted to tell their story about the Simpson murder trial on television so that they could explain to the public, some of whom might not have seen the trial, that they came to the decision to find O.J. Simpson not guilty of murdering Nicole Simpson and Ronald Goldman because there were a number of parts of the police investigation that just didn't add up to finding O.J. Simpson guilty of murdering Nicole Simpson and Ronald Goldman.

.   .   .

Now, after listening to the jurors, let's go back and reconstruct the Simpson murder crime again, starting with the police investigation at Nicole Brown Simpson's house.

Is there a possibility that someone else murdered Nicole Simpson and Ronald Goldman? Let's turn the crime around and look at the crime scene in another way. Is there a possibility two gloves were left at the crime scene by the perpetrator—one under the bush and the other by the victim's body? Could it be possible, if no one else had seen the bloody gloves, that someone had the opportunity to remove the glove from under the bush and make it look like only one glove was left at that crime scene by the perpetrator?

Let's say if that bloody glove was never found at O.J. Simpson's mansion. Would the police have had to look for other suspects? Could it be true that whoever killed Nicole Simpson and Ronald Goldman is still out there?

Let's see if we can come up with the truth as to how the murders happened. If a small Swiss knife, like the police say was used by the killer in the murder, was actually used, might not the blade have broken considering how Nicole Brown Simpson and Ronald Goldman were cut and stabbed? You might ask yourself whether the perpetrator used a different, bigger knife that might have come from some other place or business.

Let's look at all the clues. What about the bloody size twelve foreign-made shoe print found at the crime scene. Where did the perpetrator get that type of Italian made shoe? In the United States or in some other country the perpetrator lived in or visited?

And what involvement did the killer have with Nicole Simpson or Ronald Goldman? What was the motive? You might ask yourself if jealousy was the motive for killing the two people.

Now looking back into the police investigation, it was said that Ronald Goldman was just in the wrong place at the wrong time. But you might ask yourself, looking at the way the murders took place, if the perpetrator was at Nicole Simpson's house just to kill someone who was in her home, why did the killer attack Ronald Goldman? If the killer was waiting in the dark and saw Ronald Goldman coming, the killer had time to back away and wait until another day and time. That is, if the perpetrator was just at Nicole Simpson's condo in order to murder someone living in Nicole Simpson's home.

But is there a possibility the killer knew Ronald Goldman would be coming to Nicole Simpson's condo at some time that night. Is it possible the perpetrator went and waited for Ronald Goldman to walk up to Nicole Simpson's condo in the dark and then attacked Ronald Goldman in Nicole Simpson's yard.

As Ronald Goldman and the perpetrator struggled, the perpetrator cut Ronald Goldman's throat. Is it possible that Nicole Simpson then came out of the house and saw the perpetrator and Ronald Goldman fighting and that's when the killer attacked Nicole Simpson and, as Nicole Simpson tried to fight the killer back, she got the cuts on her hands.

Maybe Nicole Simpson then tried to run back into the house, but the killer hit her in the head with the butt of the knife, knocking her down. Maybe that's when Nicole Simpson fell on the steps and the killer cut her throat. maybe that's how Nicole Simpson got the blow to her head that the coroner's autopsy report talked about.

Maybe after the perpetrator hit Nicole Simpson as she tried to run and she lay on the step, the killer then cut and stabbed her some more. After killing Nicole Simpson, the perpetrator went back over and finished killing Ronald Goldman.

Now before the perpetrator left the crime scene, he left a blue knit cap and the gloves by the victim's body. It was as if the killer was leaving a message that the reason why the two people were killed—a very violent act—was revenge.

The killer then walked down Nicole Simpson's back walkway, leaving a bloody size 12 Italian shoe print going toward and out of Nicole Simpson's back gate. Then the perpetrator vanished in the dark night, escaping the crime scene without anyone hearing or seeing the killer who murdered Nicole Simpson and Ronald Goldman except Nicole Simpson's dog.

What that animal did that night I say makes Nicole Simpson's dog a real hero. He led people back to his owner's body.

If you now ask yourself who would have known Ronald Goldman was coming to Nicole Simpson's house at that time of night and who came ahead and waited for Ronald Goldman to appear and then attacked and killed two people, you might have the answer to the Simpson and Goldman murder mystery:

Who—What—Why—When

Now before we close, let me say that in every crime mystery, the perpetrator is always somewhere close by. And it is just a matter of time before the perpetrator is brought to justice.

—Ronald Williams

. . .